For Michael

Contents

Ludos

Playful Love

On Furlough

For Fiona O'R

I accidently put myself up for sale on *eBay*
whilst drinking warm cider in the garden.

What bothered me most was,
by the end of the auction,

there was only one bid of 99p
and the username was suspiciously

like a pseudonym used by my partner
in the past. I suppose it was nice of her,

but she could've upped the offer to make me feel
worth something, in these days of living outside.

Then I started to overthink—what did she want for 99p?
Was some outdoor sex on the cards?

The following week it showed signs of rain,
we started building a tepee-type tent;

the flowers were exploding and the vegetables
in the raised bed were lush, green and productive.

Caravan of Love

Our caravan wasn't always static, it often shook,
even when there wasn't a storm brewing.

Parked up on breezeblocks
behind the retired neighbour's bungalow,
their kitchen window framed
inside our big gable pane.

We made heat all year but in winter
the three-bar gas-fire was essential
and when the gas bottle froze,
he'd shake it and bring it indoors.

One summer's night I undressed,
pausing halfway to belly dance.
My top whipped off to reveal a coinless bra
and full skirt lowered to my hips.

I dirty-danced with spaghetti arms,
rotating and gyrating my hips,
shimmying my shoulders,
jiggling my breasts.

I turned my back on my love
to wiggle my bum
and there was Malachi next-door—
at his kitchen sink, staring right at me!

Well, I flung myself onto the brown carpet
roaring with laughter,
Michael joined me there giggling
and our caravan quaked and quivered.

I won't tell you about the night
the bed leg went right through the floor!

Eros

Romantic Love

Alone and Adrift

Fist unfurled, she stares
at the future
on her palm;
traces the arc
of her lifeline.

Picks out grit
from under her nails;
sees writing in the sand
of rough skin. Rubbing
fingers to thumb,

she hears long dune grass rustle;
webbed folds and wrinkled knuckles
become gentle ripples on a moonlit ocean;
whirlpools in the whorls
of her fingerprints.

Lunula on thumb nail,
a little moon
to navigate by; to find
a radius to her ulna.
To feel the warmth

of another's hand,
cupped and stroking
her cheek; a lightness
of touch, as sensuous
as a sea breeze.

Valentine

'Never Love Anyone Who Treats You Like You Are Ordinary'

Oscar Wilde

I knew not to be worried by the 21st birthday wine glass because it wasn't official. We were still learning to survey each other's ground conditions. Taking levels, only thinking about drilling test holes.

By the time we got the deeds to our first house he knew to offer up a pneumatic drill with vibrating chisel attachment to seismically scrape the damp cement from Belfast bricks. Didn't need to attach a bow to the box.

He applied for a Housing Executive Grant and turned the cheque into an engagement ring – my gift for being dust dirty. All those months I was his *Molly Malone* with wheelbarrow.

When we moved to the country, he gifted me green wellingtons from Ray Graham's Builders Merchants. Taught me how to wade through wet cement and not get stuck, after rescuing my foot from quicksand.

While the concrete began to congeal like baked custard, he presented me a handful of bright bronze coins, stamped 1996, to bury prosperity at our threshold.

After twenty-eight years, he knows my construction and design better than any structural plan. Ever the romantic, he still surprises me with gifts. This Valentine's Day he presented me a certificate, granting me ownership of one square foot of protected beech forest and the title *Lady Kane of Ardmore*.

Mania

Obsessive Love

Stalker

From the corner of an indigo sky
a crow propels like a sycamore seed—
Still, he watches.

Vixen and her kits scamper in the central reservation,
lightbulbs come on one by one. . .
Still, he watches.

A hen party plays a drinking game,
the waitress has a plunging leopard print top.
Still, he watches.

Tsunami of smoke and faces
pours from the pub at closing time—
Still, he watches her.

Walking, keys gripped between fingers,
she hears distant footsteps, stiletto
heel *SNAPS*—   the   night   sp lin ter s.

Dan the Man, 'Big Balls'

She was removing the waxy coating from one of his brandy balls by scraping it off with her front teeth. It reminded her of watching the TV show about how they made metal smoothing planes in a mould and threw them into a revolving drum with sand, to file off their rough edges.

Human rough edges
grated off by heat tempered blade—
delightful thoughts

The *'One Pound'* bag sweets were not balls they were rectangular with curved ends. In her head she could hear Dan correcting her, showing superiority, he would seethe—*That shape is called a stadium!* She rolled her eyes, flicked the sweet from one cheek pouch to the other and continued with her own thoughts.

Yes, they burnt your tongue, mildly, but they were not the same strength as those from her childhood. Or were they? Do your tastebuds grow and develop? She braced herself, positioning the sweet between the molars on the left, knowing not to use the right side because she valued her three-hundred-euro crown too much.

Pressure applied
satisfying crunch of candy
shattering into pieces

In the dark distance she watched the lighthouse beacon, the arc of its beam across the waves, the rocks and the cliffs of the headland. Hypnotised by the rhythm, she rolled the amber crumbs around her mouth and finished crunching. As she did, she looked around the bungalow. She hadn't tidied, dusted, or cleaned, since Dan left. Nor had she emptied the rubbish, washed a dish, or any clothes. She smiled knowing how upset the neat freak would've been. The healed hairline fracture on her wrist twinged and her gaze returned to the blinking light.

He would be having his tea now, sitting on the oval sofa built into the curved wall. This was the second week of him being back on duty, she was just beginning to relax. Fourteen weeks to go. Reaching for her needlework, she thought of the night before he left. He'd been so forceful in bed, several times; needing his fix before being all alone—his laptop the only way to satisfy that appetite.

Shivering goosebumps on skin
popping peat briquettes on the fire
sparks dancing like lightning bugs

The dog stretched out all her paws, making herself as long as the fireside rug before standing up, arching her back, circling three times and lying down again. The room brightened, then dimmed. Susan was glad the council had spent the money on the new community centre instead of on the replacement lighthouse lamp—the smart one that was automatic. The one that used a computer for other things than porn—like monitoring weather fronts, data transmission and system diagnosis.

Nobody
likes communicating
failures

She unwrapped another of his precious brandy balls, the dog glanced up to see if it was anything worth begging for, grunted and put her head on the hearth. Susan thought back to the beginning of their romance, twenty-two years ago. Dan had arranged a special treat every month. For their six-month anniversary he had taken her to Paris for a weekend in a boutique hotel with a view of the Eiffel Tower, where he proposed with the ring of a cola can. Everything about their relationship had fizzed, she couldn't look at him without feeling a ripple of electricity course across her body. They got married exactly one year from the first day they met. He changed instantly. It began with Dan challenging all her decisions, even things they'd agreed on together and then it spiralled. She tried to hide all the signs, especially from her parents. She'd thought about leaving but couldn't for fear of letting them down. She knew she'd been wrong when, on his death bed, her dad had told her to leave Dan and get a divorce. Before he could say anymore Dan had marched back in slamming the door and shouting that it would've been easier to find a doctor in Aldi. Susan's father passed away ten minutes later. Then Dan had had a row with her in the hospital carpark over a nail brush and their unhygienic nature.

Large pyramid of
sweety bags withheld as a statement
of retaliation

She pictured him unpacking, that first night back on the lonely
rock. She wondered if he discovered the lack of underwear, or
brandy balls, first and which he would miss most. Since he
stopped smoking, he practically inhaled sweets at the same rate
he'd sucked on the filterless fags.

Just fourteen more weeks of scrubbing, rinsing
and wringing out his own boxers every night.

Maybe he would pack his own bag in future.
Maybe she would never find out.

She stabbed the needle into calico.
She had fourteen weeks to prepare.

PHILIA

PLATONIC LOVE

Lemon Tart
For Paul, at The River Mill Writer's Retreat

Scales
    calibrated:
love & baking, both science
& art. Duck-egg-blue picket-fence
utensils and a henge of ingredients
arranged on a scrubbed butcher's block
countertop. The oven dial rotated
one hundred and eighty degrees   to the
circadian time of high alertness. He will chill
his hands in a basin of ice-cold   river-water
before rubbing-in frozen butter, the colour of
chandelier lupins, into sifted stone-ground
flour. Crisp thin pastry, crinkle lined, baked
blind until biscuit-brown.   Three zesty
lemons, freshly squeezed   through a sieve
of fingers. Eggs and cream   whisked until
voluminous like the garden euphorbia;
decorated with a   concentric circle
of almost-bursting blueberries, a
sprinkle of powdered icing;
positioned on the handcrafted
wooden table, as the perfect
welcome back
•

Bringing in the roaring Twenty-twenties
For PG and T-Bone

Black bunting in Belfast's Neill's Hill,
NEW YEAR'S EVE in art deco font over the bar.
Waiters in black & white, braces & pinstripes, fedoras & trilbies.

A crystal bowl of ostrich feathers on a lacquered sideboard.
Ceiling decorations of pleated stars and fans, gold, black
and silver helium balloons with long ribbon ringlets.

On the tables, strings of white pearls, plastic panamas,
elasticated headbands with dangling diamantes.
Lots and lots of selfie props—little cloche hats on sticks,

crowns, pointed glasses, glitter beards and moustaches.
Our pale, sad faces reflected in the wall of windows
and I think of the two endangered axolotls in the aquarium;

walking-fishes with insipid freckled faces,
feathered gills and blank wide smiles,
ambling around in circles in a fish-tank.

Here we are on the cusp of year end, new year,
on the crest of a decade, surrounded by decadence
in the crevasse of her loss. But there is no empty chair,

unless we count the bench at the end of the table
where your father sits alone,
putting on a cardboard masquerade mask

and looking like a mannequin, pulled straight out
of Burton's window. You, our friend, tried to fill the hole
by inviting the six of us to join your family, a break

from tradition, and while our bodies and personalities
are oversized it is not enough, for there will never
be anyone or anything that will replace your sister.

Through the final moments of 2019
we move places, as if playing musical chairs, to talk
to your parents, her husband, his folks and you, our friend.

And you are two-faced like Janus, except
your looking-forward-face is contorted like The Scream
and your looking-back-face has a smile

that no longer reaches your eyes.
We are trapped in a Christmas globe,
where the snow rages in a cyclone.

We dance on tiptoes, grappling for stable ground
and snatch at flitting memories
that melt like snowflakes on our cheeks.

*

*

*

On New Year's Day, I struggle out of bed
with wild hair, ruffled. On the landing window
there is the ghost-print of a bird.

The impact's velocity had thrust every speck of dirt,
every grain of sand, onto the windowpane;
leaving the splattered outline of a fanned tail,

plump breast and arched eyebrow-shaped wings.
I'm winded, slumped on the stairs, replaying in my mind
how last night, we had flocked around your mother

admiring the everlasting
engraved fingerprint on the silver heart
of her new bracelet.

Philautia

Love of the Self

To Those Who Say I Can't Sing

To have the sound for love on the tip of your tongue—
and not be able to make round oohs and long aahs.

To have the sound for love reverberating
around your skull and buzzing under
your eyelids. Bees dance, thrum, tap
and you have an itch you cannot scratch.
An itch that will render you blind if you rub;
but loss of one sense improves the others.

To have the sound for love in the hunt
for a single-sock match; look in drawers,
pulling garments away from edges.
See a ridge of downy dust growing
around divan base while spiders weave
tapestries out of corner cobwebs, then hang by a fine tread.

To have the sound for love muffled
in the womb of a small room.
The rise and fall of a chest, a baby's breath
in a warm woollen blanket. The clutch
of a finger in a tiny, clenched fist
the size of her beating heart.

To have the sound for love grow
from an ache in your belly, slowly rising
like molten honey. To feel your diaphragm
form a drum-taut sheet to bounce
sweet smooth notes up to the hive
darkness of your vaulted mouth.

To have the sound for love—
and sing!

On Mothering Sunday, March 2020

I took ten minutes to myself
to walk the esplanade at Broughty Ferry
a welcome breather, while lots of doors were closing.

Cracked my back, muscles tight from packing up
my nineteen-year-old daughter's student flat—
a holiday turned rescue mission.

I watched another mother on the beach
teaching her wee girl to skiff drakestones
on gentle waters at the mouth of the river Tay.

Mother Nature delivered me a gift.
First, I heard them trumpet news of their flyby,
then saw them skim the castle turrets.

Nineteen swans whooping overhead, against
the wrapping-paper backdrop of a cloudless sky;
feeling the under-draft of their wings on my face.

Pragma

Enduring Love

Ardenlea

This house has writing in its foundations.
Do you remember? How we buried bronze
and silver coins in the threshold and how,
just before concrete set, we scribed
our monograms inside a heart?

A view from every aspect.
Through the dining room window
there are coconut-scented whins,
thorny canopy, the perfect hide
for a rabbit warren.

Over morning coffee at the kitchen table,
we snare the hare in our sights;
sitting proud, in the middle of
a stubble field, softened by dawn mist
and a smattering of dewy cobwebs.

At evening high-tide, we glimpse
the sun-sparkled lough, perhaps
a triangular sail, or two, floating past;
as we sit on the sofa, me safely
harboured in the curve of your arm.

Belfast Hedgers

After John Clare

That first summer in our new home, we became
suburban hedgers. Wore hats to protect our scalps
but little else in the way of safety gear.
The holly hedge got the better of us, scratched our skin.

When the foliage was trimmed,
we could see the old woman's handywork.
How she had lovingly laid greenwood
to align with the horizon; woven into wattle

like the perfect willow baskets, with their sky-high
price tags in St. George's Market.
Long ago, might those glossy poisonous leaves
have been blotched with her blood too?

Storge

Family Love

No Recipe For Love

She baked the best
coconut chocolate squares—
didn't even need scales.

No need to read a recipe—
a cup of this, a knob of that,
the perfect batch was effortless.

When she couldn't swallow,
we took turns at wiping
her lips with ice-cubes.

The drip dripped, the clock ticked,
the rays shone through the blinds
and shadows moved but we were still,

still there rubbing her pastry-thin skin
with oil and combing pure white curls,
as hospital staff with invisible halos

went silently and steadily about
kneading, folding and rolling
with no need for instruction.

Lignum Vitae

i.

I open the door to the spare room wardrobe
and the sight of the stained cardboard box
stops me—I've forgotten what I was looking for.

Two round bowls inside, scratched
and scuffed by use. Wood of life,
the heaviest and hardest in the world.

Stamped to declare a No. 3 bias
and monogrammed, rings in yellow and black;
the outer—V.C. and inner—V. for Valerie.

ii.
My mother and my mother's mother
both cupped hands around polished bowls,
cradled brown feathered grain,

genuflecting to the bowling gods
before delivering the orbs
forehand across a flat green.

Prayed whilst watching them take off
and lean inward on their arc.
Urged them to *go on, go on, kiss Jack.*

Agape

Unconditional Love

Finding Her Way

Did any of the hotel receptionists look at us
checking-in and think it was odd
that we had booked a family room?

Especially the budget hotel
bedroom, where her bed
was a tiny bunk above our heads?

We toured across Scotland showing our girl
castles and lochs, libraries and campuses
but would any of the hotel lads and lassies

(just wee young things themselves)
have understood that we were happy
to show her new roads

but in Loch Ness darkness
we needed her close enough
to hear her breathing?

I watched dad and daughter both determined
that they'd caught a fleeting glimpse of the monster
in the shallows—where I had seen a floating branch.

Did the dogwalkers watching us on the beach
think it was a standard mother and daughter selfie, or might
they have wondered if it was one for the album entitled:

The Summer Before She Left

Dear Tara
After Sean Thomas Dougherty

I dreamed of you as a sleeping bumble
    in the yellow bloom of St. John's Wort

I dreamed of you as a tiny red feather, pirouetting
    from the bloody breast of the robin

I dreamed of you as a candyfloss cloud
    above a siege of cranes migrating

I dreamed of you as the mile-long uphill path
    to parliament buildings at Stormont

I dreamed of you as a three-toed sloth
    ruminating on rice leaves

I dreamed of you as the poker-straight slanted side rail
    of the library's bookshelf ladder

I dreamed of you as phosphine gas held stable
    within a glass globe at the Ulster Museum

I dreamed of you as a silver gilded skin-thin page
    of a purple bound Bible

I dreamed of you as an awful Aztec god reincarnated
    as a water-dog salamandering across sandy seabeds

I dreamed of you as a pop art heart
    in turquoise blue and emerald green

I dreamed of you as oxygen bound to haemoglobin
pumped from my lungs to each and every artery

Acknowledgements

So many of these poems wouldn't exist without my soulmate Michael and so it's only fair that I thank him first. He is always there for me, making me laugh and encouraging me. Thank you, Michael, you have the patience of a saint!

Similarly, this book wouldn't exist without my publisher, Mark Davidson who has great belief in me as a writer. Six years. and four books, means we know each other quite well – and we're still on speaking terms!

It takes a village, so I'd like to thank my family and friends. Thanks to poetry pals and my writing group, for feedback on this in the earlier stages. I'm greatly indebted to Mary Montague for her help in making this collection the best it could be – she is such a generous mentor. Appreciation is also due to the Arts Council of Northern Ireland who funded my mentoring along with other resources, including time to write. The gorgeous cover art was designed by the talented Jessica at Silverbirch Designs. Thanks to you, my reader, for reading! I hope you've enjoyed it.

I'm appreciative to the journals, and other platforms, which published some of the poems, namely: *Black Nore Review*, Corsham's StoryTown Poetry Competition, *Home* (Dreich Press), Flash Fiction Armagh, and *Lothlorien Poetry Journal*.

LOTTERY FUNDED

Gaynor lives in Belfast, Northern Ireland, with her husband Michael. They met in their late teens when they worked in the same company. They became friends and then went through a stage were when one wanted to go out with the other, the other didn't want to. So, Gaynor took herself off on holiday, to Zakynthos for two weeks, with her best friend Sarah. While away Michael realised how much he missed her and told her on her return. After six months they bought and renovated a house, then moved to the country and built a bungalow. When it got to the seven-year itch they decided to get hitched and booked a wedding in Jamaica. Only the Jamaicans started to riot over fuel costs and they had to change their plans. Michael also forgot his suit and, momentarily, Gaynor called the whole thing off. Has it been plain sailing since? Absolutely not but they still love each other and they still laugh together. He supports her in every decision she makes and even proofreads her poetry. She knows this isn't a standard author biography – if you wish to know more about her writing please take a look at her website: gaynorkane.com